Rookie Read-About® Holidays

W9-ARB-098

St. Patrick's Day

By Carmen Bredeson

Consultant
Don L. Curry
Reading and Content Consultant

Children's Press®
A Division of Scholastic Inc.
New York Toronto London Auckland Sydney
Mexico City New Delhi Hong Kong
Danbury, Connecticut

LEE COUNTY LIBRARY
107 Hawkins Ave.
Sanford, NC 27330

Designer: Herman Adler Design
Photo Researcher: Caroline Anderson
The photo on the cover shows a girl celebrating St. Patrick's Day.

Library of Congress Cataloging-in-Publication Data

Bredeson, Carmen.
  St. Patrick's day / by Carmen Bredeson ; Don Curry, reading and
content consultant.
      p. cm. – (Rookie read-about holidays)
Includes index.
Summary: Introduces the history of St. Patrick's Day and explains how it
is observed today.
  ISBN 0-516-25857-5 (lib. bdg.)   0-516-27921-1 (pbk.)
  1. Saint Patrick's Day–Juvenile literature. [1. Saint Patrick's Day.
2. Holidays.] I. Title. II. Series.
  GT4995.P3B74 2003
  394.262–dc21
                                    2003000466

CHILDREN'S PRESS, and ROOKIE READ-ABOUT®,
and associated logos are trademarks and or registered trademarks
of Scholastic Library Publishing. SCHOLASTIC and associated
logos are trademarks and or registered trademarks of Scholastic Inc.

1 2 3 4 5 6 7 8 9 10 R 12 11 10 09 08 07 06 05 04 03

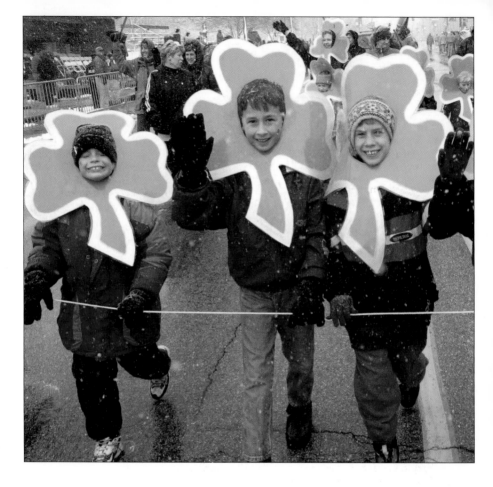

Do you celebrate (SEL-uh-brate) St. Patrick's Day?

March 2004

Sunday	Monday	Tuesday	Wednesday	Thursday	Friday	Saturday
	1	2	3	4	5	6
7	8	9	10	11	12	13
14	15	16	**17**	18	19	20
21	22	23	24	25	26	27
28	29	30	31			

St. Patrick's Day is March 17. On this day, people celebrate Ireland and the Irish people.

Ireland is an island
(EYE-luhnd) near Great
Britain. An island has
water on all sides.

St. Patrick was a Catholic priest. He went to Ireland in the year 400.

He taught the people about the Catholic religion. He helped build many churches.

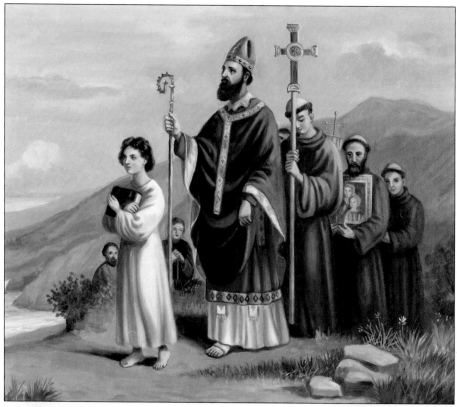

St. Patrick

7

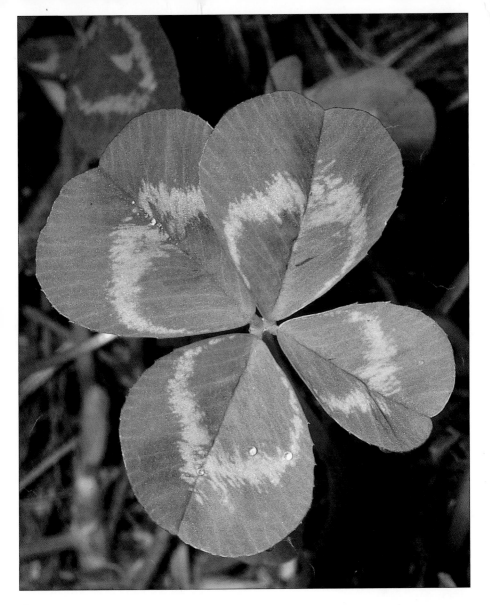

8

Some say that St. Patrick used a three-leaf clover to teach about his religion.

A three-leaf clover is also called a shamrock. Many people say that a shamrock with four leaves is good luck.

The Catholic Church named Patrick a saint after he died. A saint is a spirit that is believed to protect and help people.

More than 60 churches in Ireland are named after him.

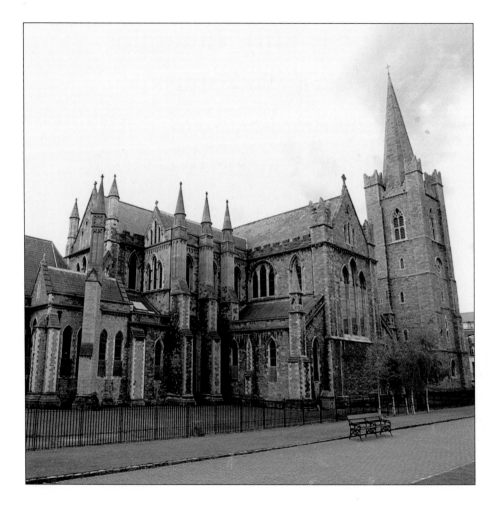

11

Ireland is called the Emerald Isle (EYE-uhl). Emeralds are green gemstones.

Ireland is called the
Emerald Isle because
the countryside is so
green with plant life.

People wear green on
St. Patrick's Day to honor
St. Patrick and Ireland.

The national color of
Ireland is green.

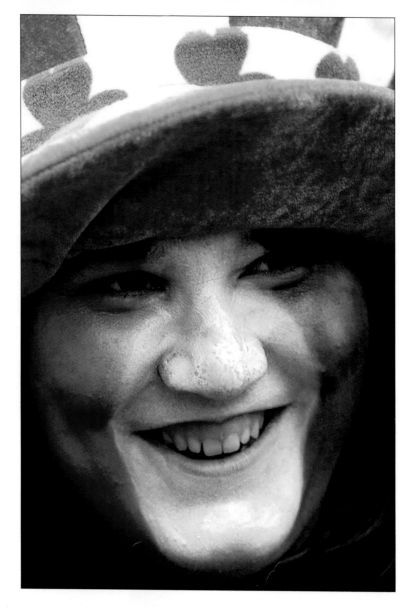

There are parades and
parties around the world to
celebrate St. Patrick's Day.

In Chicago, Illinois (ILL-uh-noy), the Chicago River is dyed green.

Some people wave
the Irish flag.

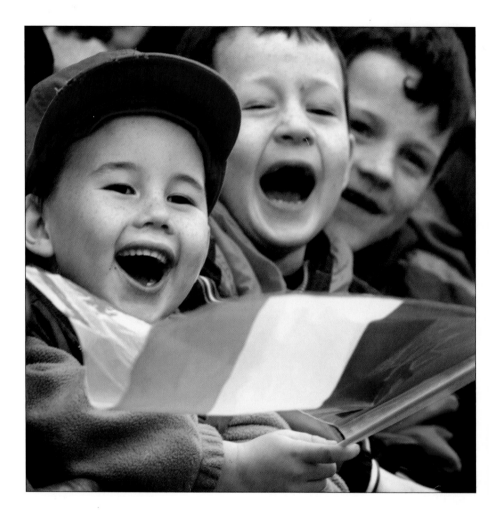

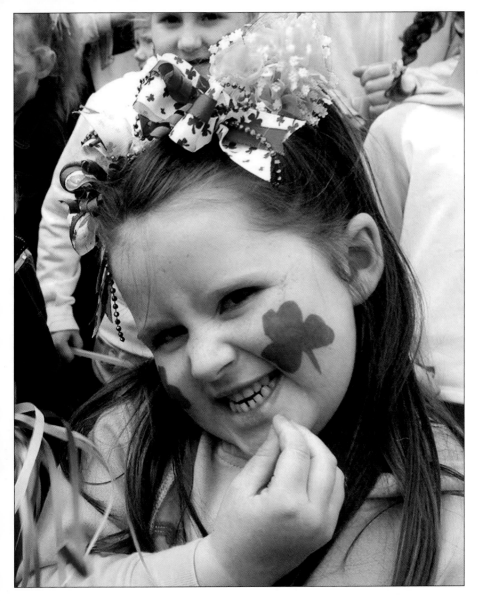

20

Everyone is wearing green!

This girl has shamrocks painted on her face.

21

Some people play bagpipes. Bagpipes are used often in Irish music.

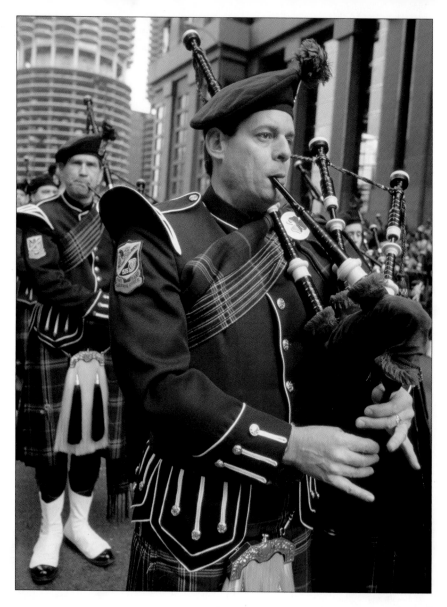

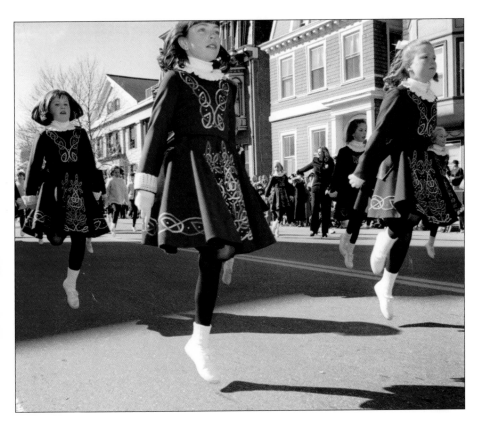

24

Dancers do an Irish jig.

Sometimes the party food is green.

How would you like to eat green cookies?

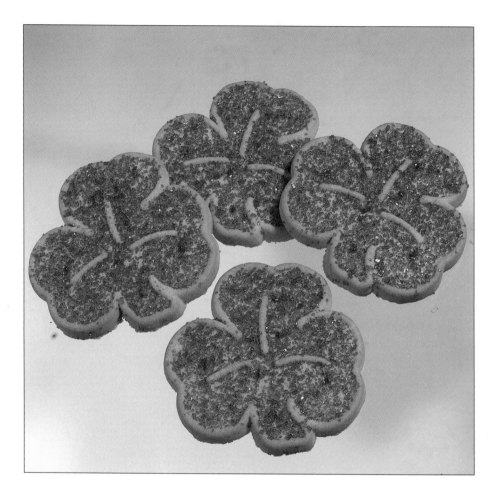

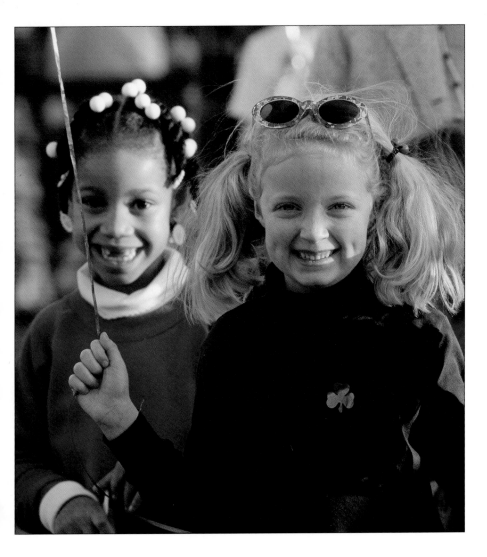

You do not have to be Irish
to celebrate St. Patrick's Day.
Anyone can join in the fun.

Words You Know

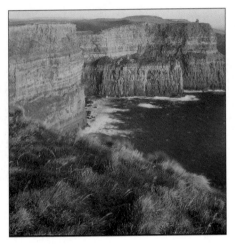

bagpipes

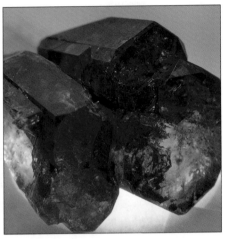

emerald

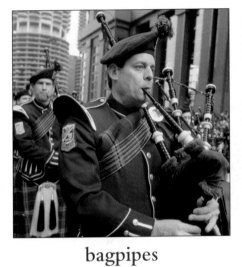

Ireland

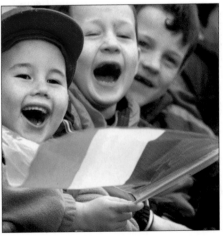

Irish flag

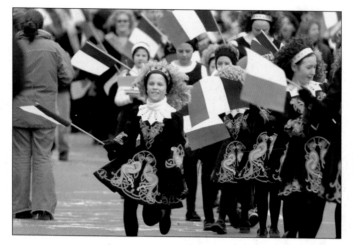

parade

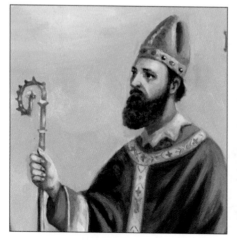

St. Patrick

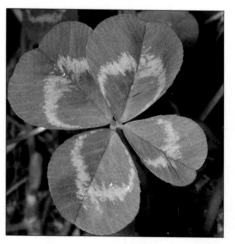

shamrock

Index

About the Author

Carmen Bredeson lives in Texas. She has written a number of books for children.

Photo Credits

Photographs © 2003: AP/Wide World Photos: 11 (John Cogill), 17 (Mike Fisher), 16, 31 top (Don Heupel), 24 (Peter Lennihan); brand X pictures/Nicole Katano: cover; Corbis Images: 23, 30 top left (Sandy Felsenthal), 28 (Kevin Fleming), 19, 30 bottom right (Reuters NewMedia Inc.); Getty Images: 3 (Liaison), 15; ImageState: 27 (Roger Markham Smith), 13, 30 bottom left (Tom Till); Photo Researchers, NY: 12, 30 top right (Carl Frank), 8, 31 bottom right (Gilbert S. Grant); Superstock, Inc./Bianchini: 7, 31 bottom left; The Image Works/Topham Picturepoint: 20.

Map by Bob Italiano